To Banish Darkness

Modern Reflections on Hanukkah

Edited by Rabbi Menachem Creditor

To Banish Darkness
Modern Reflections on Hanukkah

2018 Paperback Edition, *First Printing*

ISBN: 9781731303479

*Let the straight flower bespeak its purpose
   in straightness—to seek the light.
Let the crooked flower bespeak its purpose
   in crookedness—to seek the light.
Let the crookedness and straightness
   bespeak the light.*

from "Psalm III" by Allen Ginsberg

also by Menachem Creditor

yes, my child: *poems*

Intense Beginnings:
 Selected Writings, 2014

What Does it Mean?
 Selected Writings 2006-2013

(*ed.*) Not By Might:
 Channeling the power of Faith to End Gun Violence

And Yet We Love: *Poems*

Primal Prayers:
 Spiritual Responses to a Real World

(*ed.*) The Hope:
 American Jewish Voices in Support of Israel

Commanded to Live:
 One Rabbi's Reflections on Gun Violence

Siddur Tov LeHodot
 Shabbat Morning Transliterated Prayerbook

(*ed.*) Thanksgiving Torah:
 Jewish Reflections on an American Holiday

(*ed.*) A Manifesto for the Future:
 Conservative/Masorti Judaism Dreaming from Within

(*ed.*) Peace in Our Cities:
 Rabbis Against Gun Violence

Slavery, Freedom, and Everything Between:
 The Why, How and What of Passover
 co-edited with Rabbi Aaron Alexander

A Pesach Rhyme

Avodah: A Yom Kippur Story

Rabbi Rebecca and the Thanksgiving Leftovers

A portion of the proceeds from this book will support anti-poverty work in NYC led by UJA-Federation.

CONTENTS

INTRODUCTION

I remember, as a child, being taught that the Jewish People was called to be "a light unto the nations,"[1] a phrase that made me feel proud and responsible. But I was also taught (sometimes more by furtive glance or timid gesture than explicit messaging) that the place of a Jew in the world is fragile and shaky.

As the years pass by, I've learned again and again that both messages are true. Which is why the lights of Hanukkah are so very important.

The lights of Hanukkah are not for hiding. They defy the world-as-it-is (for Jews and every other persecuted and marginalized group) with the culminating mystical glow of eight flames, collectively pointing to the fullness of Creation's seven days - *plus one.*

Hanukkah's glow should be seen as nothing short of a piercing vision of the world to come.

The diverse voices included in this collection point the way. What an honor to have assembled them and experienced the power of their vision as part of this book's creative process. May their visions be met by willing hearts and hands. And May our world be truly illuminated, as we together increase the light.

Rabbi Menachem Creditor
Channukah 2018/5778

---

[1] Isaiah 42:6, 49:6, and 60:3

Reclaiming Sacred Space with Light
Or Chadash b'makom Kadosh
Rabbi Jeremy Weisblatt

Rabbi Jeremy Weisblatt graduated with distinguished honors from the Schreyer Honors College at The Pennsylvania State University with degrees in Classics and Ancient Mediterranean Studies, International Politics and Jewish Studies. After graduation, he began his rabbinical studies at The Jewish Theological Seminary of America, finishing at Hebrew Union College – Jewish Institute of Religion (NY). He currently serves as the rabbi of Temple Ohav Shalom in Allison Park, PA and is concurrently in a doctoral program at HUC-JIR, with a focus on Talmud, Responsa and Jewish liturgy.

And when the war was over, they returned to their defiled Sanctuary, and together, lit a new light, and the holy was found once more...I have always been drawn to the end of the story of Hanukkah. That moment when the Maccabees, surely being both physically and mentally exhausted, somehow gathered the strength to enter the Temple grounds, to raise the fallen menorah, and rekindle the holy flame.

I've marveled at, the strength of their conviction, to take back what was defiled, make it holy once more,

11

and bring the Divine light back to the world. In 2018, here in my home of Pittsburgh, this act of our ancestors provides me with the inspiration and meaning to go forth, to bring light and hope into a darkened world.

The cloud of darkness descended upon my world on Saturday, October 27th, 2018. Defilement, pain, and loss entered into our holy place. The Tree of Life synagogue went from a place filled with prayer, with light, with life, and darkened as an anti-Semitic gunman, unleashed hatred and rage, and took eleven bright lights from our world. Like our ancestors, our community became dark. Like our ancestors, our holy space was taken from us. Like our ancestors, we were confronted with the question - "*what now?*"

"What now?" It meant first facing the darkness in our world. Like so many others, I went to funerals and vigils, heard the stories of the lives no longer being lived, and mourned and grieved. I needed to confront the darkness and cruelty in our world. As *shiva* then came to a close, *Rosh Hodesh Kislev* - like a beacon in the night - arrived and the light began to slowly shine. The "what now" became clear: to use the example of our ancestors' strength and actions, as our story for how and why we could rebuild.

> "Like our ancestors, our community became dark. Like our ancestors, our holy space was taken from us. Like our ancestors, we were confronted with the question - "what now?""

It would have been easy for us to retreat. To encircle ourselves in layers of security and leave the sacred in its profaned state, allowing the darkness to claim ultimate victory. But this is not the Jewish way, for after our ancestors defeated their foes, and vanquished the darkness, they believed enough in the inherent goodness of the world, and restored the sanctuary to its former glory and light.

We can embrace the light, even in the midst of darkness, and sanctify that which has been profaned. This is the story that my community, that Pittsburgh is has embraced, for love is stronger than hate. We are rebuilding, and the defiled sanctuary in Tree of Life is slowly being reborn. The congregations are praying once more, and we are have brought actions of *gemilut chasidim* (loving-kindness) to shine the light in Pittsburgh again. From interfaith vigils, rallies, and actions of social justice, the sanctuary is not just being sanctified once more, but its sanctity is spreading beyond its walls.

Responding as the Maccabees did, not with hate, but with love, not with darkness, but with light, not with wiping away the old, but of honoring the past and rededicating it to the service of future good, this is how we build a better tomorrow. By responding to the darkness with its opposite, is the only way to stop the darkness, and create a sacred world of tomorrow.

As the memorial of Tree of Life is moved into the sanctuary, our community is moving forward. We, like our ancestors, are never forgetting the past, but we do not let it dictate our future. We, like our ancestors, are choosing to respond not in kind, but in opposition to hatred and darkness. We, like our ancestors, are inspired by light splitting the darkness. This is the path my community is choosing, this is the *derech*, the path, the Pittsburgh Jewish community is choosing, as we honor the eleven sacred lights no longer among us. We hope and act with the belief that this will be the path that our world will come to choose, so that a new light will come to shine over Zion, over Jerusalem, over Pittsburgh, and over the world.

Bringing Light in an Uncertain World
Rabbi Miriam Berkowitz
In loving memory of Randie Malinsky, a rationalist and a
woman of action, whose light continues to shine

> Rabbi Miriam (Carey M. Knight) Berkowitz, a native of
> Montreal, was ordained at the Schechter Rabbinical
> Seminary in 1998 and certified in the first cohort of
> Israeli chaplains as well as the NAJC. She is the
> International Coordinator of the Spiritual Care
> Association and Founding Director of Kashouvot:
> Pioneering Pastoral Care in Israel. She resides in
> Jerusalem where she finds her spiritual center walking
> on the Tayelet and doing pottery, in addition to
> teaching, learning and singing at several local
> synagogues.

One Saturday night in November, 1995, I was
making havdala with JTS rabbinical students
spending a year in Israel Matt Berkowitz, Matt
Eisenfeld *z"l* and Shai Held in their apartment in
Rehavia. The calmness of the evening broke down
when an urgent announcement of the tragic and
unexpected murder of then Prime Minister Yitzhak
Rabin was made on the radio.

I was numb, frozen, unbelieving. My first reaction
was to sweep the kitchen, wash dishes, clean the
counters: busy myself with mundane activities that

would prove that life goes on, no matter what. Twenty-three years later, in the wake of the murders in Pittsburgh just weeks ago, I reflect on the event and try to understand what caused me to respond the way I did.

We live in an uncertain world and worry about many things that could go wrong. We have lots of roles and much responsibility to juggle any given day. In this busy world of ours one additional event can put us over the edge. Taking a step back, distancing oneself, refusing to internalize the full impact of tragedy when it strikes and instead performing a simple, repetitive activity with a predictable outcome can be very comforting.

Reactions to disasters, whether natural or man-made, are as varied as the cultures, personalities, upbringings and communities we represent.

While the Meyers-Briggs personality scale, which divides people into 16 different personality types, has limitations, I find it a useful tool for analysis.

Sandra Krebs Hirsh & Jane A.G. Kise built on Meyers-Briggs and the Jungian types they incorporated, in their book Soul Types: Matching Your Personality and Spiritual Path. They identify four general approaches to religion/spirituality.

1. The rationalist or theologian seeks to understand the big questions through study

and analysis, to make order, to learn from the past.

2. The gathering type thrives on community, shared worship and meals, singing and socializing, which feeds their emotional need for fellowship.

3. The mystic wants to experience union with the Divine, in solitude, nature, meditation or other rituals.

4. The activist has a passion for ethical behavior, social justice and *tikkun olam*, working across cultures and borders.

We may attribute our different ways of coping with disaster to differences in culture, upbringing, and role models, or, in part, to types described above.

So how can we bring light into the world? How do we respond to crisis, and what do we do to make things even better when they are coasting and fine?

For those of us charged with expressing the collective emotion – rabbis – trying to add something when all has been said and done is sometimes challenging.

> "We live in an uncertain world and worry about many things that could go wrong ...so how can we bring light into the world?"

As a community, the Jewish people are good at addressing the aftermath of tragic events through liturgy. Whether by saying Psalms or writing personal prayers, saying kaddish or lighting memorial candles, standing vigil or attending services, we know how to mourn, to give honor, to make sure we do not forget. Some take a practical approach- sending food to a *shiva* home, caring for orphans or raising funds for refugees. Others seek to understand the root causes of the event and make sure it does not recur.

Yet on the individual level, we develop vastly divergent reactions. Some want to know every little details of the disaster that transpired, while others suffer from nightmares once they see one drop of blood. Sometimes it is just too much to fathom.

My hope is to expand the range of acceptable ways to respond to tragedy. We need all kinds. We need people ones who respond in the first hour, the first day, the first week. And we need ones who, 10 years later, are foster-parenting a child who was traumatized when disaster struck, or mentoring a PTSD sufferer.

We need people who will embrace the victims and weep with them, gather communities and give them a chance to grieve. We need those who can meditate and pray and invoke Divine mercy. We need those who are strong and seemingly unfeeling, who can write the eulogy, bury the bodies, analyze the event and understand the causes, and field the impossible question, *"why?"*

We need people who take care of practicalities and make sure the widow has a ride to her checkups and hot food for dinner, who install better metal detectors and train security guards, who educate school children about tolerance or change the gun licensing laws.

I suggest that distancing oneself from a disaster, on whatever scale, is a way of protecting oneself. Even this is a legitimate response to tragedy, whether far away or close to home.

Time gives us the distance we may need to process, to accept, to try to fathom the full scale of the disaster.

I even suggest that wanting to revenge, or being angry, embarrassed, and a broad range of other harsh emotions – are all normative and acceptable reactions. Indeed, being proactive rather than only responding to past disasters is also worthy of our time and energy.

Hopefully this resilience will not be called on again. Hopefully we will not test the limits of our wisdom, empathy, spirituality or activism. Yet if we do, we should not judge or rank the various responses, individual and communal, but rather celebrate and synchronize them.

And when things are going well, we also can also celebrate our diverse avenues toward tradition. The college student volunteering at a soup kitchen is the activist; the professor comparing manuscripts of the

Talmud is the rationalist; the post- army Israeli tracking in India or going to a retreat in the *Negev* is the mystic, and the *chavura* members sharing song and potluck dinners are the gathering, community type.

Each of us can be attracted to more than one style, or can flow between types depending on circumstances and times of life. But we do have a general preference, and organized religion might try harder to vary its offerings in order to nourish each of the groups.

A Story of Both Violence and Hope
Ruth Messinger

> Ruth Messinger is the Global Ambassador of American
> Jewish World Service, a member of the World Bank's
> Moral Imperative Working Group on Extreme Poverty,
> and the inaugural Social Justice Fellow at the Jewish
> Theological Seminary of America.

The good news is that most of us, as adults, get to
pick and choose among the themes and rituals of our
holidays. We can — in our own activities, at our own
tables, in our prayers — focus on the parts of the story
that most resonate with us and not on those that
disturb us.

At Hanukkah [and Purim] there is a powerful story
of going to and being in battle which emphasizes the
fierceness of our efforts and takes delight in
reporting the slaying of our enemies. I get that that is
part of our story. I even get that without some of
these battles and some of these victories we might not
be here, but I personally don't want to glorify war or
to send that message to the next generations.

On the other hand, I love the focus on light and hope
that is a core part of the Hanukkah story. The notion
that the oil lasted long enough to keep the *ner tamid*

(eternal light) going is a nice-size miracle at a time when there are too few of those. And the emphasis on having holy light in the Temple and on increasing the light in the menorah every night speaks to me and, I think, to others. We are reminding ourselves that the more we can find and shed light on our lives, the easier it will be to find solutions to our problems.

Also, we are recognizing that at this darkened time of year we all yearn for more light. We are nicely united with and connected to virtually every major world religion that has some holiday or ritual or custom that involves light at the low moment in the annual calendar. It reminds me of what it must have been like in ancient times to have the days get perpetually shorter and darker when there was as yet no understanding that this was a process that had limits and would reverse; how logical, if

> "...the more we can find and shed light on our lives, the easier it will be to find solutions to our problems."

you did not know that, to create some rituals that emphasized the importance of light and then to keep those to help deal with these days of the cycle.

Surely this year we can all engage in this aspect of our Hanukkah holiday with special fervor. There is too much darkness around—attacks on truth, explosion of anti-Semitism, continuing virulent racism and ugly white nationalism—and we need to see the light, to see the light increase and to do all we each can to shed more light, to be beacons and torches for change. We might do well to hold high, along with our regular prayers, the new motto of the Washington Post: "Democracy dies in darkness."

Let us light our menorahs, create more light each night and see that — and not violence or ugly nationalism — as a way out of our current morass.

Bending Light
Rabbi Dan Ornstein

Dan Ornstein is rabbi at Congregation Ohav Shalom
and a writer who lives with his family in Albany, NY.
He is the author of the forthcoming book, *Cain v. Abel:
A Jewish Courtroom Drama* (Jewish Publication Society)

Having barely passed high school physics, I
surprised myself some time ago when I took on the
daunting, thankless task of teaching a lesson about
light, prisms and rainbows for a Hanukkah program
in our community religious school. Hanukkah is a
great religious celebration of the Jewish people's
victory over its oppressors during the Maccabean
War against the Syrian Greeks in 165 BCE. Modern
Jews' readings of the story through the lenses of
minority and smaller-nation status emphasize
timeless values such as maintaining one's identity
and political freedom.

Yet Hanukkah's religious fame is also founded upon
its core legend, the miracle of the Menorah that
remained lit in the holy Jerusalem Temple despite an
insufficient amount of olive oil, after the Maccabean
War ended.

Because light is so prominent a Hanukkah theme, I reasoned that talking a little about optics with families would be a cool way of emphasizing its symbolism: white light and the spectrum as metaphors for unity and diversity, waves and particles as symbols for the spiritual and the physical, common features of science as a window on God's miracles.

What could be so hard about such a lesson, especially for an experienced, fun loving, boundary bending religion teacher like me? What fun we would all have shining lights through prisms in a dark room, watching in amazement all the pretty rainbow colors on the ceiling.

I did all the right things to prepare. I ran circles in my car around a ridiculous traffic circle to get to a science supplies store, whose stock of prisms I cleaned out for a whopping fifty dollars. "So, to teach a lesson on prisms, I guess I should just shine some light through one of them, right?" I eagerly inquired of the manager. "Uh, yeah," he responded, "That's what you do with those things." I tried shining a flashlight through a prism onto the ceiling of my well-lit bedroom, only to become frustrated that no rainbow appeared.

"*Honey*," my wife gently pointed out, "*There's too much residual light in the room. You have to do this in the dark.*"

I read all about prisms, light and refraction on Wikipedia, understanding none of it until, two days before the big classroom demo, my wife explained to me over coffee why light can be bent at an angle into its different wave lengths which we perceive as colors. *Huh*? I made posters, rehearsed the science, kept playing with

> *"...we witnessed a tiny though potent example of God's miracles hidden in such a common experience, especially at the darkest time of the year."*

my flash light and prism in my room, this time in the dark, jumping with joy, "*Yeah!*" each time the seven primary colors appeared magically on the walls. I thought about light, rainbow colors, the Festival of Lights and light symbolism until I felt like my head would explode.

The day of the program arrived. I welcomed three different groups of students and their parents, who included at least one scientist and one ophthalmologist, both of whom were on duty as parents, not professionals. Everyone joined me in in my makeshift refractive fun house, and I was completely alone.

> "What does light do when refracted and why does it do this?" I asked the older students.
> "What colors do you find in a rainbow?" I asked the youngest students.
> "Do you notice that a prism has three sides?" I asked the third, fourth and fifth graders.
> "Uh, Rabbi, that prism has five sides," one of my future Nobel Prize-winning third graders corrected me.

My science was disastrous, but we had a great time as I created rainbows on the ceiling; we witnessed a tiny though potent example of God's miracles hidden in such a common experience, especially at the darkest time of the year.

Each night of Hanukkah, I will increase the number of tiny lit candles in my Chanukiyah and watch their muted but luminous stream flow out into the darkness of winter, into the gloom of our times. I will stare at the shadows it makes on the wall, maybe try a prism trick or two to release the colors from their spectral prison. The late singer, Leonard Cohen wrote: "*There is a crack in everything; that's how the light gets in.*"

As I stand watching the light, I will try to turn his insight into a question: how can I keep light flowing through the cracks in the world that threaten to make it crumble?

Let There Be Light
Rabbi David Paskin

> Rabbi David Paskin is an accomplished spiritual leader, singer/songwriter, entertainer, Jewish futurist, social activist, award-winning Jewish educator and founding rabbi of OHEL. In 2018, David was honored to be chosen as a Rabbinic Peacemaker Fellow by the One America Movement. Prior to moving to Florida, David served as the rabbi and spiritual leader of Temple Beth Abraham in Canton, Massachusetts for seventeen years. David currently serves as the Director of Youth and Family Engagement at Temple Sinai of North Dade and the Educational Director of the Institute of Jewish Knowledge and Learning.

In 1912, a small spiritual magazine called *La Clochette* (The Little Bell) printed "The Prayer of Saint Francis," also known as "Make Me an Instrument of Your Peace":

> Lord, make me an instrument of Your peace;
> Where there is hatred, let me sow love;
> Where there is injury, pardon;
> Where there is discord, harmony;
> Where there is error, truth;
> Where there is doubt, faith;
> Where there is despair, hope;
> Where there is darkness, light;
> And where there is sadness, joy.

> O Divine Master,
> Grant that I may not so much seek
> To be consoled as to console;
> To be understood as to understand;
> To be loved as to love.
> For it is in giving that we receive;
> It is in pardoning that we are pardoned;
> And it is in dying that we are born to eternal life.

In this beautiful prayer, the verse that calls out to me at this time of year is, *"Where there is darkness, [let me bring] light."*

It should not come as a surprise that so many faiths and communities have festivals of light at this time of year. Hanukkah, Christmas, Kwanza all fall in early winter while Diwali and The Tazaungdaing Festival come just a touch earlier in late fall. At this, the darkest time of the year, people of all faiths and cultures yearn for light.

The association between darkness and depression is well established. In a 2008 study, neuroscientists at the University of Pennsylvania kept rats in the dark for six weeks.

"Just like plants are drawn to light - all creatures need the warmth of light to dispel our fears and our sadness."

They found that after this time the animals exhibited depressive behavior and suffered damage in brain regions known to be underactive in humans during depression. The neurons that produce norepinephrine, dopamine, and serotonin — common neurotransmitters involved in emotion, pleasure and cognition — were slowly dying.

Just like plants are drawn to light - all creatures need the warmth of light to dispel our fears and our sadness. And so, when there is no natural light - we create light by lighting candles and hanging colored lights.

And God said, "let there be light."

In the first moments of Creation - God too yearned to fill the darkness with light. To illuminate what would become our world and to inspire us to continue God's work of creation by ourselves, creating light.

And while the daylight hours are indeed the shortest in the winter, it is not just the light of the sun that we miss. The darkness of the winter reminds us of the presence of darkness, pain, and suffering even in the warmest and brightest of summers' days. By bringing light to the darkness of winter we re-dedicate ourselves to the sacred work of bringing light wherever and whenever there is darkness in our world.

May this season of light inspire all of us, regardless of our religious beliefs, to serve as instruments of God's creative power by bringing light where there is darkness. And may the candles of our Chanukiyah remind us of the promise of Creation and help us re-dedicate ourselves to that sacred work.

Spread the Light
Rabbi Robyn Fryer Bodzin

Rabbi Robyn Fryer Bodzin is the spiritual leader of Israel Center of Conservative Judaism in Queens, NY and Co-Chair of Rabbis Against Gun Violence. A member of the Rabbis Without Borders Network, she also serves on the Executive Council of the Rabbinical Assembly and as a mashgicha at Ben's Deli.

The Torah's instructions to Aaron the High Priest for lighting the sacred Menorah are a powerful source of contemporary wisdom. A menorah is perhaps the most universal symbol of Judaism. This 7-branched candlestick appears on buildings, products and stationery. There is a huge intricately designed menorah right across from the Knesset building in Jerusalem. Many, if not all, of us have a menorah (or its close relative the *chanukiyah*) on a shelf in our homes.

It stands proudly in synagogues. It signifies victory. And with two added branches it becomes the trademark of Hanukkah.

A menorah also appears on an arch in Rome to

symbolize Israel's defeat. Capturing the Menorah made the Romans believe they had indeed ended the Jewish nation and turned out our lights. *How wrong they were.*

What was so special about the biblical menorah? One distinction is the way that it was made. It was not put together piece by piece; first a base, then attach a shaft and then branches.

We read in the Torah:

> *You shall make a lampstand of pure gold; the lampstand shall be made of hammered work; its base and its shaft, its cups, calyxes, and petals shall be of one piece. (Exodus 25:31)*

The original Menorah was made out of one single block of gold that was beaten into shape. Three branches extended on each side, and one in the center. And the cups were shaped so as to project the light forward, not just straight up. The goal of the Menorah was to spread Divine light everywhere into the world.

"The Menorah represents our mission and our history."

In essence, the Menorah represents our mission and our history. We spread our light, and our Torah into the world. From its inception, the Menorah was always about light, and eradicating darkness. It was literally created to do away with darkness. And today it still stands, fulfilling that very mission.

Power and Transformation
Rabbi Danya Ruttenberg

Rabbi Danya Ruttenberg is the author of *Nurture the Wow: Finding Spirituality in the Frustration, Boredom, Tears, Poop, Desperation, Wonder, and Radical Amazement of Parenting*, a National Jewish Book Award finalist and PJ Library Parents' Choice selection, and six other books, including the Sami Rohr Prize-nominated *Surprised By God*. She has been named by Newsweek as one of ten "rabbis to watch," and the Forward one of the top 50 most influential women rabbis, and written for The New York Times, The Washington Post, Time, The Atlantic and other publications. She currently serves as Rabbi-in-Residence at Avodah. This piece was originally published in 2013 on truah.org and appears here with the author's and Truah's permission.

The intersection of Parshat Miketz[2] and Hanukkah invites us to reflect on two different ways in which transformational impact can be effected, and the importance of understanding the nuances of each.

We see two drastically different models of power and change in these stories. In Miketz, Joseph—an

---

[2] Genesis 41:1–44:17.

Israelite foreigner in Egypt who, by happenstance, is granted an audience with the Pharaoh — manages to land himself a high-ranking job in the royal court. His power is extraordinary; he controls the Egyptian storehouses during a time of famine. He could well have chosen to be highly selective in his rationing to Pharoah's subjects, and he could have chosen not to offer the bounty to foreigners as well. He could have made a myriad of decisions that could have shored up Egypt's intra- or international power, created tactical advantages over neighboring nations, or simply concentrated the grain-as-wealth for himself and those within his inner circle. And yet, he makes the decision to work for the benefit of as many as possible, opening the granary to Egyptians and foreigners alike, for the overall flourishing of the region. He is an outsider to Egyptian society, but he is able to work within the existing systems and power structures to benefit a large number of people in concrete and important ways.

And yet, this method would hardly have worked for the Hasmoneans. In the 2nd century, the Judeans lived under a repressive regime. The Syrian king Antiochus IV attempted to control the population by repressing their practice of Judaism — forbidding *brit milah*[3] and Shabbat observance, for example — and defiling the Temple with sacrifices of swine. The oppression was acute, with no real place to go. Of course, some Judeans chose to comply with the king's edicts, but they didn't change the system so

---

[3] The ritual of circumcision.

much as attempt to get by within its stifling dictates. The moment of truth came when a small bandit army rose up in resistance and, against all odds, managed to overthrew the foreign rulers, leading to a period of national self-determination known as the Hasmonean dynasty.

(It's worth noting for the record that the Hasmoneans themselves didn't necessarily rise to power without their own atrocities — whether that reflects the perpetuation of cycles of trauma, the corruption of power, regional norms of the time, or something else, I can't say.)

Here, there was no great gig to be gotten in Antiochus IV's court that would have made a meaningful difference in the lives of the people suffering on the ground. Sometimes we can appropriate the system. Sometimes we have to blow the system up.

There isn't one right answer, of course. And sometimes, in order to create a radically new paradigm, we need both — those lobbying the halls of Congress and those

> "With each step we take towards creating the change that needs to be, we serve God."

protesting loudly outside the Capitol. It is our task, as people working to create better, safer, more just lives for all, to be attuned to the nuances of opportunity. When is this a moment to try to enter the system and push it on its own terms, according to its own rules? When is this a moment to go outside the system entirely? In what role will my talents and passions best be served? There are myriad paths towards justice, and with each step we take towards creating the change that needs to be, we serve God.

What Miracle?
Rabbi Brent Chaim Spodek

Rabbi Brent Chaim Spodek is rabbi of the Beacon Hebrew Alliance. He has been recognized by the Jewish Forward as one of the most inspiring rabbis in America, Hudson Valley Magazine as a Person to Watch and by Newsweek as "a rabbi to watch." He is a Senior Rabbinic Fellow of the Shalom Hartman Institute and a Fellow of the Schusterman Foundation.

Hanukkah, the eight-day holiday of lights. It's the simplest and most complicated of holidays and it functions in America in ways that are virtually impossible to predict from its history.

On the most basic level the traditional practice is to light a chanukiyah (or menorah) at sundown on each of the eight nights of the holiday. The chanukiyah is placed in a window or some other public place so that the miracle can be publicized. Which miracle? We'll get back to that.

People spin dreidels, eat foods fried in oil like donuts and of course, exchange gifts with their loved ones. For reasons that have far more to do with its coincidental occurrence with Christmas, it also has a huge pop-culture footprint – check out for instance, Adam Sandler's (dare I say – classic?) Hanukkah Song, parts 1 to 4.

On a historical level, the holiday is a celebration of the victory of Jews over their Syrian Greek conquerors in 164 BCE.

Way back then, the Greek empire brought new ideas and institutions to the Middle East, and in the land of Israel, many Jews embraced these developments. Democracy is great! Bath houses are lovely!

Jewish reformers wanted to merge these two cultures, so they assimilated parts of Greek culture into their own, taking Greek names like Jason, exercising in the gymnasium and prospering within Greek institutions. By the way, I'm an American born rabbi with a Celtic name writing in English, so these issues are not altogether alien to me, nor, perhaps, to you.

But not all Jews assimilated. Some resisted quietly, practicing and learning Torah in private, while others fled to the hills and waged their own form of cultural resistance, which the Greeks were happy to ignore.

After a few years, the Greek spirit of toleration ended for some unknown reason. The Syrian Greek king, Antiochus IV, issued a series of decrees defiling the

Jewish Temple and banning Jewish practice under penalty of death.

So, as in any good action movie, a ragtag army of rebels emerged to fight the empire. Judah Maccabee, led an insurgent revolt fighting against the Greeks and the Jewish reformers with equal ferocity. Ultimately, and perhaps miraculously, the small group of rebels did defeat the Empire. Yes, Star Wars analogies are entirely appropriate here.

So we return to the question -- *What's the miracle of Hanukkah?*

In some ways, the miracle was the military victory of the tiny band of guerillas insurgents against the hegemonic Greek empire. But the later rabbinic tradition, which formed Judaism as we know it, focused not on the fighting, but on the spiritual one – when the Maccabees regained control of the Temple they cleaned and purified it, but there was only enough oil to light the ritual candelabrum for one night. That little cruse of oil miraculously lasted eight days, hence eight days of Hanukkah.

So really, we have both the military miracle and the spiritual miracle. Your choice. But that's not the end of the story.

On a personal level, Hanukkah can actually be quite challenging. The heroes of the story can be seen as religious freedom fighters and a model of liberation.

However, this revolution, like many others, reserved its greatest fury for moderates, in this case, those who sought compromise between Greek and Jewish culture and therein lies the essential contradiction of the American Hanukkah.

American Hanukkah, is nothing if not an attempt to strike a compromise between Jewish culture and surrounding American culture. In a traditional Jewish framework, Hanukkah is actually a relatively minor holiday, perhaps like Arbor Day in an American context. It has become a major juggernaut only because of its proximity to Christmas in the American calendar.

> "The miracle I celebrate is the ongoing transmission of a story inherited from the past and transformed so as to nourish us in the present."

Countless Jewish children see the beautiful lights and trees of Christian friends and neighbors and ask, *"Where are our lights?"* It is to answer that question, the chanukiyah (or menorah) has become the major symbol we know today.

As a liberal American rabbi, who proudly and deliberately draws on my American heritage for some things, such as notions of individual liberty and gender equity and my Jewish heritage for others, such as a focus on the Divine, collective concern for the poor and the importance of spiritual practice, I see the power of learning from multiple heritages. That means I might very well have been one of the

Hellenized Jews who the Maccabees sought to destroy.

When I light my chanukiyah in a few weeks, the heroes I will think of will be yes, the warrior Maccabees who resisted oppression, but even more so, the rabbis who 500 years after the Maccabee revolt, retold the story and shifted the emphasis to the spiritual miracle of unwarranted hope and the oil which lasted for eight days. They inherited a story of military victory and re-imagined it, holding onto the past with one hand and the present with the other, so as to live a Judaism that was both authentic and meaningful to them. More than anything else, the miracle I celebrate is the ongoing transmission of a story inherited from the past and transformed so as to nourish us in the present. As the rabbis of the Talmud inherited and transformed, so too do we, and pray that so too will our children and grandchildren

May all our Hanukkahs and all our lives be both authentic and meaningful.

Seeing the Dark in a Different Light:
The Power of Our Language to Promote Racial Justice
Rabbi Dev Noily

Rabbi Dev Noily serves as Co-Rabbi of Kehilla Community Synagogue in Piedmont, California. Rabbi Noily's piece was originally published in 2016 on truah.org and appears here with the author's and Truah's permission.

The Black Lives Matter movement has re-focused my attention on the ways that I participate in the racial injustice that is pervasive in our society and culture. One of those ways is through language — both what I say and what I hear. And especially, the ways that I use "light" and "dark" as metaphors for "good" and "bad" or for "hope" and "despair." In these subtle and not-so-subtle ways, our language constantly delivers the message that lighter is better than darker, that white is holy and black is corrupt or bereft of holiness. This week's Torah reading creates an opening for Jewish sources to guide our use of language in different direction–as a path to liberation and justice.

The Torah portion Beha'alotecha[4] begins with Moses passing along G-d's instruction to Aaron to light the lamps of the menorah, and with Aaron actually kindling the lights. The medieval commentator Ramban (Nachmanides) links Aaron's lighting here to the menorah of Hanukkah. He reads this kindling as an allusion to the "miracle" of the Hanukkah menorah, brought about by Aaron's descendants, the Maccabees, many generations in the future.

The earth's movement around the sun also connects Beha'alotecha with Hanukkah. This year we read Beha'alotecha during the week of the summer solstice in the northern hemisphere. For those of us in the north, this week brings the year's longest stretches of daylight and its shortest nights. Six months ago, during Hanukkah, the opposite was true. It was the winter solstice here, and our nights stretched out long and dark as the daylight retreated.

Hanukkah is especially susceptible to metaphors that fail to challenge, and that can reinforce the racial injustices of our time. One recent Hanukkah, I was surprised by a piece that T'ruah circulated which began, "We often use metaphors of light and darkness to speak about hope and despair, or human rights victories and human rights abuses,"

> *"Darkness is associated with the generative state that precedes birth."*

---

[4] Numbers 8:1–12:16.

and then went on to build on those metaphors as a source of spiritual teaching.

When I contacted T'ruah to respond, I was invited to offer this d'var Torah. So with gratitude and respect, and in the spirit of a *machloket l'shem shamayim,* an argument for the sake of heaven, I offer some Jewish teachings that present alternatives to these metaphors. And I invite you to join me in considering practices that can help us bring our language into greater alignment with our aspirations for racial justice.

Rabbi Arthur Waskow writes about Tisha B'Av, the day that commemorates communal loss and creates space for collective mourning:

> It is the heart of summer: hot as a furnace, dry as the tomb. A shower, a breeze, are forgotten memories. The earth is panting in exhaustion — almost as if the birthing of her harvest has gone awry, as if the birth-pangs will go on forever but there will be no fruit. And people are exhausted too. Their freshness and fertility, warmed and renewed by the sun of spring, has wilted as the sun grew still hotter. We feel burnt out. The whole world is being put to the torch. (*Seasons of our Joy,* p. 207)

Waskow offers a striking and powerful alternative to our dominant metaphors. Here, it is the excess of light and heat that is frightening, dangerous, and imperiling. The saddest, most devastating time of the

Jewish year comes not in the darkness of winter, but in the scorching heat and relentless light of summer.

The rabbis of the Talmud spoke about Torah as "black fire on white fire" (Palestinian Talmud Sotah 8:3), where the black fire is the letters themselves and the white fire is the space between them. Both transmit meaning, and if we had only one without the other, there could be no Torah.

Darkness is associated with the generative state that precedes birth. Just as the Torah's creation story begins with *"darkness on the face of the deep,"* (Gen. 1:2) so too our lives begin in the womb–the darkest, most protected and most nurturing place we may ever know.

Our traditions and sacred stories are laden with opportunities to challenge the dominant metaphors of light and darkness that reinforce negative racial stereotypes and perpetuate racial injustice in our society. As the solstice approaches, may we celebrate the light of our long summer days, and celebrate, too, the deep winter nights unfolding for our siblings in the southern hemisphere. One could not exist without the other.

Hanukkah and the Light of the First Day
Rabbi Fred Guttman

> Rabbi Fred Guttman has served as the rabbi of Temple Emanuel in Greensboro, North Carolina from 1995 to the present. From 1979 to 1991, Rabbi Guttman lived in Israel and served as the rabbi and principal of Alexander Muss High School in Israel. He has been the chair of the Israel/Foreign Affairs subcommittee of the Commission of Social Action for Reform Judaism and has been instrumental in helping draft several significant Union for Reform Judaism resolutions, including resolutions on torture and human rights.

The Talmud teaches:

> "Our Rabbis taught: When Adam, on the day of his creation, saw the setting of the sun he said! 'Alas, it is because I have sinned that the world around me is becoming dark; the universe will now become again void and without form — this then is the death to which I have been sentenced from Heaven!' So he sat up all night fasting and weeping and Eve was weeping opposite him. When however dawn broke, he said: 'This is the usual course of the world!'" (BT, Avodah Zarah 8a)

For all of us, darkness can be frightening. How does one even begin to overcome the fear of darkness?

Many years ago when I served in the Israel Defense Forces, we were on maneuvers in the Negev wilderness. The expanse was breathtaking. One night, we took a broom and cleaned off a piece of earth that was about twenty by twenty feet. The next morning, we went out to that patch and observed all sort of animal tracks. This was very near to where we were sleeping. There was always a guard, but the guard was not aware of the animals. Yes, the Negev can be full of life, but the animals use the darkness for their own security.

The lesson for us was that we needed to not fear the darkness, but learn how to maneuver within it. We learned that one small light, or striking a match, could enable the enemy to see us and could cost us our lives. So we learned to trust the darkness instead of fearing it.

Yet as the Talmud passage above shows that most of us are afraid of the darkness. If we are at home, we might not lock our doors during the day, but we usually lock them before we go to bed at night.

> *"The lesson for us was that we needed to not fear the darkness, but learn how to maneuver within it."*

This is a month of great darkness, more than any time during the year. Therefore perhaps it is no accident that both Judaism and Christianity seem to have holy days which stress light over darkness.

I am convinced that darkness has a dual quality. It can be something which can provide dread or security. Might it be the same with the light of day? Our task is to attempt to turn both darkness and light into something which is not dual.

Maybe this was what the prophet Isaiah had in mind when in reference to the future he taught:

> "No longer shall you need the sun for light by day, nor the shining of the moon for radiance [by night], for the Lord shall be your light everlasting, your God shall be your glory. Your sun shall set no more, your moon will no more withdraw; for the Lord shall be a light to you forever." (Isaiah 60:19-20).

In the world as we know it, night and day alternate ("And there was evening, and there was morning," as Genesis repeatedly puts it). However in Isaiah's vision, the light of day and the darkness of night will both be replaced by the light of God. The duality of day and night will give way to the unified light of God.

The light of God is indeed very different from the light of day or the darkness of night. The light of God is created on the first day of creation. The light of the sun and the moon, of day and night, of darkness and light, was created on the fourth day. So what happened to the light of the first day?

Perhaps this is the understanding of the writer of Psalm 97 who writes. "Light is sown away for the righteous." Some interpreters feel that the light referred to here is the light of the first day, not the light of the sun or moon.

Similarly, the author of Proverbs teaches: "The soul of man is the lamp of God," (Proverbs 20:27). The Hasidic master R. Yehuda Leib Alter of Ger (1847-1905), known as the Sefas Emes takes this even further. In his mind, the task of the Jew is to become like a star of God, bringing God's light to the places of darkness. He teaches: "A human being is created to light up this world."

Elsewhere, the Sefas Emes asks why on Hanukkah, we celebrate a miracle involving a very small drop of oil. His answer is "In those days the menorah remained lit through the tiny drop of oil they had. And now, too, there is a small point in every Jew." This small point of light within each of us has great potential. It may be small but on Hanukkah we are challenged to make it larger by bringing it into actuality, bringing the light of God within to the world outside.

As we enter this dark time of the year, let us be cognizant that our task as Jews is not simply to light Hanukkah candles, but to become candles, beams of the light of God, beams which are seeking to replace the duality of day and night with the unity of Gods compassion, justice and love.

As you light the candles, may you be ever aware that our fundamental challenge is to draw forth the light within us, the light of the first day, the light of God, in order to turn the world as it is into the world as it ought to be, a world filled with the light of God!

Reclaiming the Darkness: A Piyyut
Karen Erlichman

Karen Lee Erlichman, D.Min, LCSW provides psychotherapy, spiritual direction and mentoring in San Francisco, integrating spiritual practices and body-centered resources to support healing. She is is a senior consultant for Ethics of Care and Resource Development for The Dinner Party and the People's Supper, as well as a faculty member in the Jewish Spirituality D.Min program at the Graduate Theological Foundation.

Darkness is not something to be banished. Because of racism, darkness is associated with evil, danger and negativity. I pledge to refrain from language that associates darkness with evil. I commit to honoring the sacred spark that rests in the beauty of darkness.

To reclaim darkness is to rescue it from the paradigm that prizes whiteness and lightness over the magic and mystery of the dark. Darkness is a holy space that begs reclaiming.

Blue night sky darkness
reveal the radiant moon and stars.
Dark brown soil of earth that smells
of the pungent spicy promise of new life.

Dark green blue depths of the ocean.

Darkness of chocolate, coffee, plums and purple eggplant.

Darkness as *HaMakom* - the place we go when our eyes are closed, when we pray, when we sleep and dream.

Sparks of light can only be seen with the backdrop of darkness. When the light is too bright, the spark is imperceptible.

Blessed is the Beloved One
who created darkness and light.
I pray that we rest
in the lap of Your Shadows and Light.
May we inhabit and sanctify
the twilight spaces
in between darkness and light –
the emerging sunrise
and the dimming light of sunset.
God of All that Is,
bless us
with the expansive darkness
of peace.

Adjusting the Historical Spotlight, Returning to Stories of Women's Heroism

Tehilah Eisenstadt

Tehilah Eisenstadt is an educator-activist, speaker and early-childhood education consultant. Tehilah has written curriculum for multiple Jewish institutions, and Cordoba House, a Muslim religious school. Her multi-faith advocacy and educational leadership centers on empowering and safeguarding children, particularly girls. Tehilah received an MA in Jewish Education and an MA in Midrash from The Jewish Theological Seminary. Tehilah serves as Director of Education and Family Engagement for SAJ, in Manhattan.

As an educator, and mother, with no ties to Nigeria, the idea of 276 children whisked into oblivion left me shaking. The perpetrators, an all male-led terrorist group named "Western Education is a Sin," inevitably saw a school of girls well on their way to becoming educated women, likely to educate their villages and future families, as a call to action. The terrorists removed their greatest threat and turned them into multi-use assets. Girl-students became cooks, cleaners, sex slaves and forced mothers.

57

The night I read the news from Chibok I cried out to my fellow female religious leaders and organizers for action I couldn't even conceive. We have gathered a multitude of times as Christian, Muslim and Jewish women, giving voice to girls who were silenced. Over four years later, 112 girls remain with their captors and Bring Back Our Girls NY (BBBOGNY) still raises the alarm and we pray, daily. When 276 black girls are a blip on the world screen we indirectly teach girls, especially black girls, how easy it is to erase female bodies and stories.

A year after the Chibok girls' abduction, I sat in my preschool Director's office, overhearing the filming of a class video. Each child came to the hallway stage to recount a story they learned over the past year. A trend unfolded, while boys chose from several narratives, girls chose from the only tales of women they had heard that year: Miriam or Esther.

Women's stories matter, girls' bodies stolen anywhere affect those girls and their families for generations, their stories also affect the girls who register the world's reaction or distraction to these stories. This is why colleagues from BBBOGNY gathered mid-2018 to find a new way forward. As women of faith we were tired of the never-ending apathy to women and girls bodies used as battlefields. We sought ancient religious and modern texts to help us understand the scope of this narrative. In preparation, a friend shared the tale of Channah Maccabee. In this elaborate Midrash, it is Channah Maccabee who provokes her brothers to battle. Both Channah and Judith, by unusual measures, change their men-folk's throwing up of hands into fiery action.

Yeshiva educated, with a master's degree in Jewish Education and master's degree in Midrash, I was never taught these stories. Now, as an activist-educator, I aim for a balance and diversity in the characters we teach. Among the many challenges this poses, the heroines of Hanukkah are not PG-13 material. Channah Maccabee and Judith the widow warrior follow in the tradition of Queen Esther, which goes back as far as our matriarch Sarah. In Jewish ancient tradition we women use our bodies to save our family, or our entire people. Afterwards we are often erased from the story, or our role is downplayed. It is hard to talk about how these female battles were fought and won.

How do we rework female Jewish narratives of heroism without reinforcing that female power can only stem from manipulation of the male gaze? How do we share these challenging stories? Our ancestors asked themselves similar questions when engaged in the political bind of wanting to celebrate Hanukkah under foreign rule. As some scholars explain, highlighting the story of a little jar of oil was more prudent than celebrating the story of a successful Jewish rebellion. As a people, Jews have navigated thorny narratives before. I trust that we can return Channah, Judith and their sisters throughout our texts and history to our Jewish narratives with as much will and wisdom. We begin by teaching our adults these stories. Together educators, clergy and parents will find a multitude of ways to swing the spotlight back towards women's heroic actions.

When we bring ancient narratives of women from obscurity into light, wisdom and possibility is illuminated. This illumination occurs for girls, women and for all people who once could only find themselves by squinting at the margins of history.

Be the Shamash
Rabbi Jesse M. Olitzky

> Rabbi Jesse Olitzky serves as rabbi and spiritual leader
> of Congregation Beth El in South Orange, NJ. A native
> of New Jersey, he previously served at the Jacksonville
> Jewish Center in Jacksonville, Florida, before returning
> to his Jersey roots in 2014. He is a part of the South
> Orange-Maplewood Interfaith Clergy Association and
> the Newark Clergy Affairs Committee. Additionally, he
> is a part of the Maplewood Police Department-Clergy
> Alliance, working to build a more just community.
> Additionally, he serves on the Rabbinical Assembly's
> Social Justice Commission, as a JOIN for Justice
> Rabbinic Fellow, and as a CLAL LEAP Fellow. He is
> passionate about justice, the Baltimore Orioles, and
> spending time with his wife and three children.

The Chanukiyah, the Hanukkah Menorah, serves
more than just a ritual purpose. We are taught that
when we light the Menorah, we should place it in the
window for all to see. By doing so, we fulfill the
mitzvah of Pirsum HaNes — of publicizing the
Hanukkah miracle. During the winter solstice, at the
darkest point in the year, the flames of the Menorah
add light to the darkness.

The Talmud mentions how Rabbi Shammai and
Rabbi Hillel debated the proper way to light the

Menorah. But regardless of their differing perspectives, there was universal agreement that you use a shamash, a helper candle, to light all the other candles. To this day, the shamash is on a different level than all the other candles of the Menorah, emphasizing its significance.

We look around the world and it is easy to be consumed by the darkness of society. But doing so means that we forget the miracles that surround us every day. On Hanukkah, we don't only celebrate the miraculous military victory of the Maccabees, or even the miracle of oil burning for eight nights. The miracle of Hanukkah is to appreciate the miracles in our lives, despite the darkness that we all too often may feel or experience.

When we celebrate the miracles in our lives, no matter how large or small they may be, we also understand our responsibility to be a metaphorical shamash. With each day, the light of the Menorah increases, until all nine candles (including the shamash) burn on the final night of the festival. The use of the shamash reminds us how easy it is to light up the darkness. Just as the light of the shamash spreads to other candles and quickly illuminates the night, we must also be the initial spark to illuminate the darkness, helping to inspire and enlighten others.

May we appreciate the miracles of old and the miracles in our everyday lives. And may we never stop trying to light up the darkness.

The Resilient Child Within
Rabbi Craig Scheff

Rabbi Craig Scheff has served as rabbi at Orangetown Jewish Center in Orangeburg, New York since his ordination from the Jewish Theological Seminary in 1998. Craig also serves the Rabbinical School at JTS as Adjunct Lecturer in Professional Skills and as a member of the Rabbinical School Council.

The nine year-old Israeli boy with the large soulful eyes stands alone on the stage, his teacher-counselor-accompaniast off to the side on a stool. The youth looks totally relaxed, the microphone a therapeutic pet in his hands.

The strings begin to reverberate their introduction and the child opens his mouth to sing. Time stops and the tears begin to flow from the eyes of the teachers, therapists and foster parents in the audience. The group of resident at-risk children gathered as a makeshift audience put their arms atop each other's shoulders and begin to sway side to side. The boy's sweet voice ascends and descends like angels on a ladder, and with it our souls soar, almost out of control with the swing of our emotions.

Knowing that the boy's biological parents are not present, that the child has suffered emotional abuse (at the very least), that at a tender age his life is broken in so many ways, and that but for the presence of the caregivers in the room he might be totally lost, it is no surprise that the group is overcome with emotion in hearing his sweet and powerful voice. But to understand his Hebrew words in the moment is to be filled with awe, appreciation, inspiration and hope:

> *"Be not afraid to fall in love,*
> *That the heart may break,*
> *Be not afraid to lose along the way.*
>
> *To get up every morning*
> *And to go out into the world*
> *And to try everything before it ends*
>
> *To search from whence we came*
> *And in the end always return to the beginning*
> *To find yet more beauty in everything*
> *And to dance until overcome*
> *By exhaustion or love."*

(Lifnay she'yigamer, The Idan Rachel Project)

Resilience has been defined as the power to be able to recover readily from adversity or challenge. And it is one of those human traits that I consider to be among God's greatest gifts.

For a week in November on a volunteer mission in Israel, seventeen of our community members witnessed the power of resilience. We saw resilience in the ability of an abused child to sing before a crowd of peers and strangers; in the work of Yoav Appelboim, the executive director of Kfar Ahava Youth Village who sees too much suffering, yet continues to make meaningful improvements in the lives of so many; in a society that resumes school and work a day after rockets rained down on its homes; in a kibbutz (Hannaton) that has reinvented itself to stand as a beacon of religious pluralism and an advocate for societal change in the face of extremism.

We saw the resilience in ourselves: in our ability to make the sacrifices of time and resources to do the work that takes us out of our comfort zones year after year; in our willingness to suffer the emotional toll of being inside the suffering of children; in sharing the pains of loss, memory and empathy inside our own community family.

We saw resilience from afar, as the natural elements wreaked havoc across the ocean, from fires on the west coast to snow on the east coast, and families abandoned homes to survive and begin anew, and individual acts of kindness and sacrifice eased the burden of others.

There is something within the human spirit that enables us to get up every morning, to go out into the world, and to try everything before it ends. Despite the disappointment, despite the pain, despite the knowledge that we may not complete our task and that our hearts may be broken yet again. To me, there is nothing more miraculous or more divine.

I've heard it taught that the true miracle of the Hanukkah oil is not that what was enough pure oil to burn for one day lasted for eight. The more miraculous aspect of the oil story may be found in the Maccabees' willingness to kindle the light at all! After all, some might have hung their heads in disappointment and frustration, surrendering to the futility of lighting a lamp that might only burn for a short while. Instead, the Maccabees prove to be a model of resilience, combining their faith and self-reliance in their commitment to fight back the darkness, if only for a day.

The holiday of Hanukkah reminds us "to dance until overcome by exhaustion or love." Its light is a reminder that we have been granted a divine gift to draw upon when we think we can't take one more step, can't suffer one more loss, can't survive one more broken heart.

Oh, by the way, the little boy with the angelic voice? His name happens to be Or, meaning light. And as is his name, so is he. May he always know it, and may he always be.

And may we always recognize our own light of resilience within.

The Light of Day
Asher Witkin

Asher Witkin is a singer-songwriter currently studying Contemporary Music and Creative Writing at Columbia College Chicago. His previous vocal work includes singing back up for Coldplay, Kehlani, Daveed Diggs, and The Stone Foxes. His debut album 'Becoming Home' is available now! Asher is also an experienced wearer of mismatched socks.

It surprised me how little enthusiasm I felt when it came time to vote in the primaries last March. I had gone to dozens of protests, followed every twist and turn of the Mueller investigation, and watched countless segments of late-night talk shows trashing the President and his party. Yet when it came time to vote, and for the first time no less, the whole thing felt rather anticlimactic. Gone was the rush of righteous anger. Gone was the excitement of criminal charges and court room drama. Gone was the pleasant hum of watching a show dedicated to telling me what I wanted to hear.

I needed some form of ID with my address on it to register, which I didn't have. I could have requested a document from my school, but I would have had to go pick it up in person. It all just seemed like a lot of work. In the end, election day came and went, and I never cast a ballot.

The Maccabees never faced this problem. It takes a kind of bravery and valor to fight on a battlefield that I simply do not possess, but for the average American today, the fight against darkness does not require battle strategy or an ability to defend oneself against an elephant attack. We are faced with a different problem: the wars we have to wage are just kind of boring.

Admittedly, it's a privileged problem to have. All things considered, I'd rather call my senator than engage in guerilla warfare, but it is a problem nonetheless. When it comes time to do the day-to-day work of making the world a better place, I often just can't find the drive.

Intellectually, I know that donating to charity, calling my representatives, being conscious of my effect on the climate, supporting ethical businesses, and voting, are a few of the most important ways I can help to make my country better. But I just can't get truly excited about any of them. I want to march in the streets. I want to watch breaking news. I want to give passionate speeches about politics. And all of those things matter! But they only matter insofar as they can inspire real action.

Banishing darkness in this country, in this age, requires an ability to fight battles we will never see won in our lifetimes. It requires empathy deep enough to feel the relief of people whose names we will never know. It requires the humility to acknowledge that much of the work that needs to be done is not glamorous and will never be recognized. It's easy to write an essay for a book. It's harder, at least for me, to do the kind of work that never becomes a compliment, never finds its way onto a plaque or into history.

I don't have an answer for how to will myself into engaging in these kinds of Mitzvot, but I know that if I allow myself to believe I'm doing my part merely by sharing angry posts, joining marches, watching the news - even writing an essay – I will have sold myself short. Judas Maccabeus could never have restored light in the face of darkness without countless men and women who risked their lives knowing they would never be remembered. This Hanukkah, I'd like to do a better job of acknowledging them, and I'd like to do a better job of taking actions to banish darkness that will never see the light of day.

Not by Might, and Not by Power
Rabbi Neal Joseph Loevinger

Rabbi Neal Joseph Loevinger is a rabbi, chaplain, kosher supervisor and proud parent in Poughkeepsie, NY, the Queen City of the Hudson.

The spiritual lessons of Hanukah aren't only in the stories of the Maccabees and the flask of oil, but also in the texts our sages chose for synagogue reading during the holiday. To wit, on the Shabbat of Hanukah our haftarah, or prophetic reading, is from the prophet Zechariah, who lived at the time when the Second Temple was being built (about 520 years before the common era) after the first exile. Zechariah has a great vision of a rebuilt and restored Temple service, so it's easy to see how that connects with Hanukkah, which recalls and reenacts the rededication of that same Second Temple a few hundred years later. In particular, at the end of the haftarah, in Zechariah 4, there is a vision of a golden menorah (lampstand), which again provides an obvious connection to Hanukkah.

Digging a little deeper, there's a somewhat subtler verse which explains the vision of the menorah:

> "This [the preceding vision of the golden menorah] is the word of the LORD to Zerubbabel: Not by might, nor by power, but by My spirit — said the LORD of hosts. Whoever you are, O great mountain in the path of Zerubbabel, turn into level ground! For he shall produce that excellent stone; it shall be greeted with shouts of '*Beautiful! Beautiful!*'" (Zech. 4:6-7)

I imagine you're now asking: *what's a Zerubabbel?* The answer is: not a what, but a who. Zerubbabel was the grandson of an earlier king of Judah, and he himself was a leader of the community that came back from exile and started working on the Temple. Thus, when the prophet says that the vision of the menorah is a word to Zerubbabel, it means that the prophet is conveying to the leader of the community a vision of what he must do, along with encouragement that he can accomplish it.

Note that the Temple and its lights will be rebuilt *"not by might, and not by power, but by My spirit."* Some have seen in these words a subtle hint on the part of the ancient rabbis that however much we might admire the Maccabees, we ought not rely on military means to secure redemption for our people. That argument probably made a great deal of sense in the time of the Roman occupation of Palestine but it's probably a moot point after the establishment of the State of Israel.

Another quite beautiful interpretation of "not by might, and not by power" comes from Rabbi Samson Raphael Hirsch, who lived in Germany in the late 1800's. He says that this prophecy teaches that when our efforts are oriented towards holy ends, we should never be discouraged:

> "Let every human circle know, every individual person, even the outwardly weakest and smallest, that as soon as he is penetrated with My Spirit, and thereby places himself in the service of justice, brotherly love, and holy living, he has the strength of giants in accomplishing his work. . . ."

With this interpretation, what was in Biblical times the work of building a physical structure is expanded to include all who toil to create a more sacred world. It's not by physical might or power of any kind that the Divine Presence is made real to us, but by openness of the soul and orientation towards the Holy. That's a great message for Hanukkah: that our work of justice and compassion is not held back by the fact of our being ordinary, flawed human beings. We can accomplish great things with nothing more than humble and open hearts- and thereby bring light to the world.

Toward a More Sacred World
Dasee Berkowitz

> Dasee Berkowitz is the director of Ayeka's Becoming a
> Soulful Parent program to help parents and Jewish
> institutions change the conversation around parenting
> – from a doing mindset to a becoming one. Dasee has
> over 20 years of experience working in informal
> educational settings in the US and overseas in Israel,
> India and the FSU. She has served as an educator and
> consultant to many national and international agencies
> including AJJDC, Makom and the JCC Association and
> most recently has applied her educational expertise to
> community settings, building prayer experiences that
> nourish connection between parents and children,
> through her work with 92Y Shababa and Kehilat Zion
> in Jerusalem. Dasee writes about soulful approaches to
> parenting in Kveller.com, JTA, Forward.com, Haaretz
> and Times of Israel and is passionate about engaging
> and supporting parents in their challenging and sacred
> role as parents.

She sleeps a lot. The all-day kind of a lot. After 95
years of living, feeling tired accumulates. She wakes
up at night, wandering the halls of her nursing home
facility. She wonders what she should be doing.
Those who work at the facility invite her to sit down,
to drink something. She likes apple juice the best.
From the outside, the light has gone out from her
eyes. I am not sure she recognizes this 46 year-old

granddaughter. Her voice sounds like there's gravel deep in her throat. She tells me, everything hurts.

Her dementia is real. She doesn't know where she is and what she should be doing. "Am I in someone else's house?" she will ask, as she pulls the quilted white covers over her shoulders lying in bed. I pull up a chair next to her and look, bearing witness to her life. I hold her hands, caress her skin. It's thin and soft. I see past her disheveled hair and hunched shoulders. I wait to see a light of recognition. And I do, in moments. Like when she saw me today. "*Hello darling*," she sang. Her Anglo-Indian accent was like a balm to me.

The light of my grandmother's life is fading. In these short visits, infrequent by necessity because of the miles between us, I am trying to hold as much of her dwindling life in mine. I climb onto her bed and hold her gently. Her skin is thin, delicate and prone to sores. I am flooded with memories of sleeping next to her as a child, during the times she visited us from Israel. My parents didn't allow it but each night I climbed down the stairs of our suburban split level home and climbed into her bed, the rainbow quilt warming us both. The next morning she would tell me with a smile that I kicked in my sleep.

Her light is fading maybe only by my standards of light and darkness. In her bed, in this nursing home, I bless her need to sleep and to turn inward. She is no longer able to engage in the Technicolor world that she once did. The one that burst with a life filled with grandchildren and great-grandchildren. Now, simple black and white lines are all her eyes can take in. My attempt at simple conversation feels absurd. 'Would you like a cookie?' or 'Do you want to see pictures of my kids?' An eyebrow rises about the cookie and I feed her a small piece. She has interest in very little now. Instead, she is returning to something more elemental. Touch, song, faith.

"God will be with you now when you feel alone, my beautiful Nana," I say to her by way of a soft lullaby.

As winter approaches, the shorter days, and longer nights make darkness more palpable. Each night of Hanukkah, the light of each candle - one, and then another, and then another, for eight days - starts to illuminate the dark spaces around us. These candles are fragile, temporary and filled with fiery glory. Our soul, each one of us, is like a candle - fragile, temporary, unique and filled with elemental fire that has so much capacity to give off light. And eventually, with the passage of time the light dwindles. But there is fire that remains. Proverbs teaches us, *"the soul of each person, is God's candle, searching all the inward parts"* (Proverbs 20:27). By turning inward, closer to the end of our time, God's candle is with us, still searching.

When we light the Hanukkah candles we are commanded not to use them for any utilitarian purpose but to bear witness to them (*aiyn lanu reshut l'hishtameish b'hem elah l'rotam b'lvad*). It is a deep lesson to me now. Our job is to encounter each person, each soul no matter where they are in their lives or how strong their fire and to honor their light, to bear witness and to bring deep presence to them.

My teacher, Rute Yair Nussbaum, shared the kabbalistic notion that Hanukkah is a holiday connected to the Hebrew letter, *samech*. The *samech* is a round letter without end. It is the letter version of a hug, a continuous cycle in which light and darkness and light and darkness appear and reappear in our lives. We are present for life's oscillating pattern. And when life gets too dark, we can bring light, insight, enlightenment. That's also a part of our work.

As I sit with my grandmother, I am filled with presence, connection and tears that make my heart that is breaking open feel whole. Our Chassidic masters taught, there is nothing as whole as a broken heart. When a heart breaks open it allows everything in.

Our humanity can hold it all. We might just might need more practice.

Hanukkah Lights and Shabbat Lights
Rabbi Dina Shargel

Rabbi Dina Shargel has a B. A. in music from Brandeis University and rabbinical ordination from the Jewish Theological Seminary, where she also earned an M. A. in Bible. Since 2004, she has been serving as Ritual Director at Temple Israel Center of White Plains, NY.

Hanukkah is called the Festival of Lights (hag ha-urim) because its central ritual is the kindling of candles. On the first night of the holiday, we light a single flame. With each successive night, the number of lights is increased by one, so that on the eighth and final night the Menorah is filled to capacity. The effect is dramatic, as is the message it underscores: the triumph of the spirit and the victory of right over might. Shabbat too is linked to light, but its character is quite different from that of Hanukkah. Let us consider the weekly rituals of light and then return to the Hanukkah lights.

Havdalah

Light is a prominent entity in the biblical story of Creation. In fact, it makes its debut at the very beginning of the Torah, where the creation of light is God's first task in establishing order in the world (Genesis 1:2-5). Our ancient sages must have wondered what happened when Adam and Eve experienced darkness for the first time, a subject on which the Torah is silent. Here is a summary of a passage from *Midrash Tehillim* (on Psalm 92):

> When the first human beings saw the sun go down (for the very first time), the sight of darkness enfolding creation filled them with terror. God took pity on them, and inspired Adam with the divine intuition to pick up two stones, whose names were "Darkness" and "Shadow of Death." Adam rubbed them against each other and discovered fire. With great joy, he uttered a spontaneous prayer, blessing God as *borei me'orei ha-esh* ("Creator of firelight").

The blessing that the Midrash ascribes to Adam is the centerpiece of Havdalah. Interestingly, the rabbis mandated that Havdalah may be performed only after the stars, the little lights in the sky, begin to pierce the darkness. Kindling the multi-wick Havdalah candle is a ritual re-enactment of the first created entity. The large flame inspires us, as it did Adam and Eve in primordial time, to banish night-terrors and to express gratitude to God. In the glow of the flame, we gesture with our hands to witness the contrast between light and shadow. Through Havdalah we emulate God, who began the original week with light. The ritual also helps us make the transition from the holy to the mundane - bolstered by the fact of our agency - for we too can create light

- and also in God, our source for protection throughout the week.

Shabbat and the "Light of God's face"

As Shabbat is ushered out with fire, so is it ushered in. Just before sundown on Friday night, we kindle two individual candles to welcome Shabbat. Their beauty helps to set a mood appropriate to the Day of Rest – of joy (*simcha*) and delight (oneg*). At the Shabbat table, another ritual invokes light in a subtler, poetic way: the *birkat kohanim* (the Priestly blessing), recited with outstretched hands, usually by parents to each of their children (though it can be offered to others as well). *Birkat kohanim* asks for no less than the light of God's very face to shine upon its recipient – signifying Divine grace (hein) and peace (shalom).

Shabbat Lights and Hanukkah Lights

The blessings over the Shabbat and Hanukkah candles are almost identical because they follow the same formula: *asher kiddeshanu be-mitzvotav v'tzivanu lehadlik ner shel Shabbat/Hanukkah*. ("who has sanctified us with the mitzvot and commanded us to kindle the light of Shabbat/Hanukkah"). However, the two rituals are fundamentally different. The Shabbat lights function as a tool for enhancing the weekly celebration of rest and peace. Tradition bids us to place Shabbat candles on the table as a centerpiece. The focus is inward.

Though the Hanukkah Menorah is also lit at home, its focus is outward. The proper place for the Menorah is not on the table but in the window. The rabbis even forbade the use of Hanukkah lights for practical purposes. Their job is to publicize the miracle and to embody the holiday's central message: that the weak can prevail over the mighty and the spirit over the sword, and that our hopes for a better world, as improbable as they may seem, may yet be possible to realize. These are lessons to be shared proudly with others. May they inspire us to work both with our fellow Jews and with the other inhabitants of this precious earth we all share, for its betterment and for ours.

Shabbat 21b
Aryeh Einhorn

> Aryeh Einhorn is a current Lishma Fellow at the
> Conservative Yeshiva in Jerusalem. Aryeh is currently
> co-authoring a Mussar parshah commentary, but also
> occasionally dabbles in poetry. This is Aryeh's first
> poem ever published.

1
I've always preferred Beit Shammai
because who wouldn't want to compare
the contraction of the lights of
Hanukkah
to the diminishing sacrifices of Sukkot?
The essence
being
as we get closer to the boundary
between this and that
the light condenses
until
we are left with the One
perfect
bright
light
at the end
The diminishing bulls
and the final one
perfect
sacrifice,
and my People
left closer to the One
than at almost
any other time.

2

Yet we follow Beit Hillel
who instead compares
the unfolding lights of
Hanukkah
to the increasing days of the past.
The essence
being
as we get closer to the boundary
between this and that
the light expands
until
we are left with the One
perfect
bright
light everywhere
that at the beginning was small
The zimzum
the starting point
that spread
making the whole thing
(light from darkness)
about elevation
of sanctity:
Creation.

A Meditation on Light One Candle- Hanukkah and Mental Illness
Matan Koch

> Matan Koch is a teacher, consultant and thinker, who advocates universal inclusion, the idea that the best approach to inclusion of everyone is the same for those with and without disabilities, i.e. helping to eliminate barriers so that everyone can share their light. He developed these ideas as a senior disability official appointed by President Obama, prior to which he had graduated Yale College and the Harvard Law School, and spent time practicing law. A longtime student of the intersection between Judaism and Disability, Matan is proud to be admitted to the Hebrew Union College-Jewish Institute of Religion, where he hopes to combine these passions in service to the Jewish people as a Rabbi.

We all feel the darkness that encroaches as we approach the winter solstice. Some say that the reason that Hanukkah, and the winter holidays in so many cultures, have themes of light is a collective cultural opportunity to banish this darkness, or at least hold it at bay. And what a beautiful image, a family clustered around brightly burning candles, singing songs of triumph and exchanging gifts and gelt, their glow, both literally and figuratively pushing away the winter gloom.

A pretty picture, and yet, as a person who lives with depression with a strong seasonal affect component, I often feel the darkness encroaching somewhere around Labor Day, really grabbing hold as the Jewish month of Cheshvan begins. By the time we kindle the lights of Hanukkah, it takes more than the stirring words of Peter Yarrow's *"Light One Candle"*, my favorite Hanukkah song, to keep the lights from going out.

Even as acknowledge this, I am intrigued by what we can learn from the fact that the Jewish response to darkness is to gather together to kindle light. How can we collectively help to bring some light to the dark place where so many of us living with mental illness still reside? What are the candles that we can light?

With thanks and apologies to Peter Paul and Mary, I propose the following:

> 1. Light one candle to remind to listen as intently and creatively as we can for the ways that our friends and loved ones asked to be supported, from a hug, to a phone call, to a simple affirmation, and do so, to the best of our ability.
> 2. Light one candle to honor the tireless mental health professionals who support so many of us, with treatment, with teaching and with research.
> 3. Light one candle to honor the peer mentors and supporters who share their own experience and use it to guide and support those who are still finding their own best way through.

4. Light one candle as a call to advocate beyond the aspiration of mental health parity in the Affordable Care Act, to an expansion of services and coverage, providers and networks until everyone receives the necessary mental health care

5. Light one candle in memory of all of those who suffered and died in the horrific institutions of ages past, and all those awaiting a physical or metaphorical safe place in the decades since they were eliminated without replacement services.

6. Light one candle in honor of all of those who come out with their experience of mental illness, to enlist allies, and strengthen and embolden the rest of us to share our truth.

7. Light one candle for all who are suffering in silence, afraid to even share the truth of their mental illness, let alone seek help, for fear of personal or professional consequences.

8. And light one candle to bind us together, supporting each other and rededicated to fight until light is brought to us all.

The story of Hanukkah teaches us that a small group, dedicated, can be a light in the darkness, signified by the sea of tiny candles that becomes a brilliant light. The sum total of the darkness may be huge, and we may be small, but together we fight it, one candle at a time.

A portion of the proceeds from this book will support anti-poverty work in NYC led by UJA-Federation.

Rabbi Menachem Creditor is the Pearl and Ira Meyer Scholar in Residence of UJA-Federation New York.

Named by Newsweek as one of the 50 most influential rabbis in America, he has authored 15 books and has been a featured contributor to media outlets including The Times of Israel, the Huffington Post, and The Daily Forward. Rabbi Creditor is the founder and chair of Rabbis Against Gun Violence and serves as a founding advisor to the One America Movement.

A frequent speaker on Jewish Leadership and Literacy in communities around the United States and Israel, he served for more than a decade as spiritual leader of Congregation Netivot Shalom in Berkeley, California, a Trustee of American Jewish World Service, co-chair of Shalom Bayit, and sits on the Social Justice Commission of the Rabbinical Assembly.

Find out more at menachemcreditor.net

Made in the USA
Middletown, DE
28 November 2018